In Service Of Thee

Poems from the Objects Around Us

Aabha Soni

India | USA | UK

Made with ❤ on the BookLeaf Publishing Platform
www.bookleafpub.in
www.bookleafpub.com

Dedication

To the invisible in the crowd,
To the unheard in the sound,
To the forgotten little doubts,
And to the things that always see us.

Preface

This book was born from a moment when I noticed people in a robotic state—those who feel unseen, almost invisible to society. I sensed the heaviness we all carry, the constant search for validation, the quiet longing for someone to simply whisper, "It's okay."

Then I noticed the objects around me—my pillowcase, which had quietly absorbed so many tears; the office table, where many promotions were denied. I wondered—what if they, too, wanted to comfort us? What if they desired to be more than just things that just serve us?

And from that wondering, a voice began to blossom. A voice that might belong to the universe itself, speaking through everything around us—seeing us, understanding us, and reaching out in its own gentle way.

Acknowledgements

This book came from a some place inside me, and I couldn't have brought it to life without a few people—seen and unseen.

Thank you to all those who sat with me during the hard parts, even when there weren't any right words. To my family and friends—thank you for your patience, your gentle nudges, and so many other things that carried me through. To my editor, publishers, and readers—thank you for giving this book its wings. And strangely enough, thank you to the quiet corners of my room, my office desk, and yes —even my pillow—for holding space when I couldn't.

Lastly, to anyone who feels unseen or unheard—this book is for you.

Quotidian

For the ones who cry in solitude
For all the silent places ever
viewed
For the heart that just wanted to
be seen
For the souls who got lost in
passing streets

Car

I, car, am speaking from the side of the road.
I see people charging me for standing—
Although it is thy master who left thee.

I, car, am listening to radio music.
I see people honking over me for being loud—
Although it is thy master who sad thee.
Master also feels abandoned today,
After thy father shouted at him.

Master listens, cries, and feels.
Master went with me to school,
Thy father used to drive me.
Now, this pain, I witness quietly.

I, car, am here, wanting thee to heal.

Bowling Pin

I, bowling pin, am surrounded by sounds—
Some thy shouts, some thy frowns.
For I see newbies turning to masters,
And some thy daddy's little daughters.

I, bowling pin, stand tall till I fall for applause,
For thy claps when all ten of us drop.
For I see archnemeses turning into partners,
For defeat of some greater evil power.

I, bowling pin, do not complain of hurt,
For I'm deployed here for fun of thee.
Once saw thy proposal on hitting strike three,
Once, a fight amongst old family money.

I, bowling pin, observe all sorts of time.

Train Seat

I, train seat, take thee to destinies—
From newlyweds to the recently deceased.
I hold a lot of random memories.

Even when thou art nowhere near me.
I still keep up my poise,
For things may rest,
But I am always in toil.

I, train seat, am often complained about,
Blamed for the wrong positioning.
Still, I manage to journey thee throughout.
After years of wear and tear,
I acknowledge each scar in sight—
So thy master feels comfortable.

I, train seat, will bear it all, each night.

Office Badge

I, office badge, am celebrated when new,
Then slowly thy master forgets the hue.
Although remembers thee each morning,
Keeping thee aside while working, office timing.

I, office badge, notice master sigh.
Each year, thy hands wrinkle signifies.
Thou dost not understand the cause,
So, thou just hang by the place of pocket watch.

Master, I hope thy spark still ignites—
For thou art more than work defines.
Nothing to commit today is still alright.
I, only, office badge, do not ask updates of thee.

Extension Board

I, extension board, lay by cubicle side.
Thy master just working, and sighs.
Nothing—just another task aligns.

I, extension board, perceive sometimes.
How thy master is left behind,
While others are chatting and prying.
Thy sits serious, and sometimes cries.

I, extension board, hear conversations
From the other side of the block—
Wondering, would it hurt thy feelings?
Others modelling plans, hiding it from thee.

I, extension board, observe just from afar.

Birthday Candles

I, candle, hold but little memory—
For I am brought forth for a momentary story.
Yet I capture each wish ere I'm blown,
A fleeting flame, yet never alone.

I, candle, notice the glimmer in thine eyes,
When thou wishes for joy or a puppy surprise.
I witness the breath that trembles in fear,
When the future feels heavy, and doubt draws near.

I, candle, see the past holding thee tight,
Making thee wary of swift passing nights.
But I, candle, carry more than desire—
My flame brings hope, strength, and quiet aspire.

I, candle, wish thou happy birthday.

Innocence

For the ones who just learned to
smile
For shoulders weighed down by
duty awhile
For the kids who grew up too
fast
For the moments that quietly
shaped our past

Tiffin

I, tiffin, am holding healthy food,
Thy schoolmates, though, flip me off crude.
When thy observes in fear and sighs,
They ask thee to do tricks—jump high,
Buy ten rings, or skip one leg at a time.

I, tiffin, am stuffed warmly into bags,
But thy still feels cold, alone, and dragged.
They come again, calling thee names,
Mocking softly, yet with harsh flames—
Like how thou isn't tall enough to reach
Their pedestal of pride, their senior speech.

I, tiffin, find it hard to understand,
What joy thence found in bullying thy hand.

Lego Set

I, Lego set, am sitting in the corner of thy room.
I do not see in darkness, but I hear sounds—
Thy parents are fighting, abusing again,
Over something that is pretty small.

I, Lego set, am just many pieces of toy.
Funny how thou build me up, joining me,
But could not simply sort things out—
Putting each guilt, each mistake deep buried,
Never understanding what's within.

I, Lego set, am colorful and lively,
But I see the dullness within my thee.
Innocence should not be kept in storm
Or in sugar-covered relationships.

I, Lego set, am just thy escape—
From love too sharp, too hard to reshape.

Swing

I, swing, am owned by the most innocent crowd.
I keep my poise, hanging, even when no one's around—
Waiting for thee to just play with me.

I, swing, am keeper of countless laughter:
Thy stubbornness, thy sadness, thy desire.
I watch thee grow and walk away from me,
So I try not to hold any bad memory.

I, swing, have witnessed the most whimsical fights—
Over whose turn it is to have my ride.
Thy parents' eyes shimmer with unspoken love,
When thy master swings with wind up high.

I, swing, will wait till thee grow big and revisit.
I will honor thee with my wear-down wishes.

Night Lamp

I, night lamp, shall narrate thy story—
One of deep pain, and a search for glory.
For thou was a child, a child with dreams,
Orphaned by birth, learning in quiet streams.

I, night lamp, saw each one depart,
And thou, unchosen, bore a heavy heart.
Thou vowed to rise, though but a kid—
Too wise for age, too weak 'mongst others hid.

I, night lamp, never let thy spark die,
I burned each night, as thou lay nearby.
Thou studied hard, won college, won grace—
Scholarship earned, carved thine own place.
Thou became an industrialist, an entrepreneur,
Strong of will, steady and pure.

I, night lamp, now rest in thy mansion—
A token of past, of thy quiet ascension.

Scooty

I, scooty, choose the worst time to stop—
When thy child is late for the school drop,
When thy train is just leaving the platform,
When thy interview nears its final form.

I, scooty, remind thee at such time
Of the essence in being late—of life's rhyme.
Each lost moment births another seized,
A new tale to tell, an old one released
From the beginning.

I, scooty, now park and turn cold,
Urging thee to kick-start, to be bold.
Thou shalt reach thy destiny—I remind.

Watch

I, watch, am a family heirloom,
Something to give thy direction—
And a lot of unspoken strength.

I, watch, carry too much weight—
Not of material, but of responsibilities,
Of being given uptight,
Maintaining thy ancestry pride.

I, watch, am passed down in graduation,
A reminder that time
Holds and heals, passing each line.
Stand strong, be resilient.

Clutch me if thy breaks—
It will be alright

Identity

For the souls who search the
mirror in doubt
Hoping to find someone they still
recognize
For the ones bent beneath
society's mold
Till they break, then fold, then
silently hold

Sink

I, sink, am firmly placed on the wall.
It is okay to confide in me and talk.
I have seen thee breaking down,
When people in the house shout around.

I, sink, will wash all guilt down,
After thou hast eaten in absurd amount.
It is okay to be so overwhelmed—
Thy food becomes thy only friend.
But thou punishes thyself with it,
Inducing pain is a miserable thing.

I, sink, will cover all the wounds—
Just keep breathing, I know thou could do.

Towel

I, towel, am drying in the wind,
Thy mistress, grooming up herself,
Forgetting how beautiful she already is.

I, towel, am a colorful piece of cloth.
Thy mistress cried again while in bath—
Scrubbing her skin, causing bruises.

This world, this society, leaves too many bruises,
To fit into perfect, artificial muses.
Thy insecurity is just a marketing scheme.

I, towel, wipe off water and tears.
Someone with such a princess heart
Is simply just falling apart.

Closet

I, closet, am reorganized every season—
Thy scars thyself again, teary vision.
"Not being too thin," thy says,
Ranked the fattest in thy family's gaze.
Some serious pre-teen shaming.

I, closet, am full of XL clothes,
Body too big to feel beautiful,
Topic too taboo to talk about.
Esteem too low to walk away from.

I, closet, am just stuffed upon—
Another piece added to the "what if" side.
What if thou loses 10 pounds or more?
What if thou feels confidence somehow?

I, closet, come in all shapes and sizes,
But beauty doesn't depend on these disguises.

Poison

I, poison, am a woman's choice of revenge.
I take great pride in my working ways—
A slow kill down the gut for thee,
Or a fast, no-pain—thee is set free.

I, poison, am an element of secrecy.
Use me cautiously, use me wisely.
For thy was suffering, breaking vigorously—
That's when I was summoned for thee.

I, poison, may not seem to care much,
But I too feel happy when avenge is done.
Justice may find cruel ways to end—
I, poison, still will showcase my best.

Bangles

I, bangles, represent the secrecy of marriage.
People assume thy mistress to be well—
But home never felt safe to thee.

I, bangles, come in all forms.
Thy love to pair me so diligently,
Only to take me off with tears, painfully.

I, bangles, remembers that one dark night,
When thy husband broke some of me—
But thy mistress was the one
Who shattered in pieces silently.
With tortured eyes, she wanted to flee.

I, bangles, no longer wanted to shine;
I too was hurt, just like thee.

Endearment

*For the blind dates that ended in
silence
For the maybes that turned into
definite no
For the hearts that find it too
hard to trust
For the ones meant to be—
together, yet alone*

Third Date Sweater

I, sweater, hold a special place in thy closet—
Taken out on unique times.
Love is felt sweeping on thou skin,
When I slide on to make souls align.

I, sweater, am held with tender thought,
With hope this date will go long.
I witness thee with tears sometimes,
When no call is made on the return drive.

I witness thee with reciprocal love,
When thou art hugged, surprised from behind.
I, sweater, am as unique as thee—
Radiating crafted love each time.

Petrol Stand

I, petrol stand, witness heartbreak tonight,
I hear thy thoughts, loud in the quiet night.
Thou knew it's over—he's not the one,
When he said, "I'm not the conversation type, hon."

I, petrol stand, feel the weight of the words,
As thy hopes fall, unseen, unheard.
The chatterbox within thee shuts down tight,
Thy efforts wasted, lost in the night.

"But he seemed interested," thee did recall,
"Only when others made him stall."
So typical of guys to leave things unclear,
Giving just enough to keep thee near,
But never enough to calm thy fear.

Candle

I, candle, burn softly as I see
The smile fading away from thee.
The guy on the phone is hurting thou—
Even comfort feels like knives' edge now.

I, candle, provide a faint light,
As the conversation falls into night.
He's still in love with someone else,
And thou hope to smile,
Despite the pain that swells.

I, candle, carry a comforting warmth,
But thou crave it in human form.
A long hug, a comforting pat—
I do not think this is too much to ask for that.

Coffee Table

I, coffee table, love to be a part of café,
Love to captivate the moments, as thy say.
Thy mistress, thy master met for the first time—
Air breezed, heart fluttered for lovable sight.

I, coffee table, provide space to talk,
As thy master sat down so nervously.
Thy mistress asked, "Your favorite color be?"
With no pause, thy said, "Yellow."
"Are you complimenting my dress?" asked thee.

Thy sighs, smiles—with warmth, thy says,
"I never noticed colors in any way,
Till you came dressed in sunshine,
And I knew it was yellow all along."

I, coffee table, witness start of love—
Held hands, awkward shyness, souls intertwined.

Bedsheet

I, bedsheet, hold on to thy emotions
As thy longs for someone in commotion.
Thy whispers in thou drifting dreams,
Someone holding thee among reeling gleams.

I, bedsheet, witness thee say soft prayers
For love, for care, for hope, and fears.
Thy holds on for the perfect one,
Little does thy know—it's just a thought begun.
Nothing real to be longed for.

I, bedsheet, am afraid of what's in thy core.
Thy tries to bring fictional men to these fields,
Real and earthen, where no dream shields.
Believing someone will medicate perfectly,
Over thou naked scars, so desperately.

Solace

For all the bitterness we've
carried through
For the nights our eyes swelled
with cries
For the prayers, the screams, the
silent pleas
For the soft souls who knew they
couldn't flee

Pillow

I, pillow, am thy best friend.
Thou comes to me each day's end.
A tired workday, or complex love—
I welcome thee with a long hug.

I, pillow, soak up thy tears,
When thy love was unrequited fear,
When thy workload was too much,
When thy self-esteem dropped by hunch.

I, pillow, will always wait for thee—
Another trouble, or another victory.
It is okay, it is alright,
There is a sun after each stormy night.

Necklace

I, necklace, am a gift to thee—
From the sweetest best friend
That will ever be.

I, necklace, brought tears to eyes,
In receiver and giver disguise,
For thy saw the care hidden,
The way they heal each other, unbidden.

I, necklace, am no diamond jewel,
Yet thee cares for me more than gold,
For I signify a bond never growing old.
Two hurt creatures found each other,
No experience—just support one another.

I, necklace, am a proud metaphor
Of pure friendship bloom forevermore.

Crossroads

I, crossroads, wait here for thee.
I see lovers and enemies meet,
I note where many destinies lead,
And hear both nature and city's beat.

I, crossroads, witness thy journey—
A resume clutched for a job interview,
A ring held close for the perfect proposal,
An ice cream melting as a child's hand,
A skateboard driving down the street.

I, crossroads, am always waiting for thee.

www.ingramcontent.com/pod-product-compliance
Lightning Source LLC
Chambersburg PA
CBHW071236140726
47996CB00007B/2627